OAKLAND ATHLETICS

BY ANTHONY K. HEWSON

SportsZone
An Imprint of Abdo Publishing
abdobooks.com

abdobooks.com

Published by Abdo Publishing, a division of ABDO, PO Box 398166, Minneapolis, Minnesota 55439.

Printed in the United States of America, North Mankato, Minnesota.
102022
012023

Cover Photo: Thearon W. Henderson/Getty Images Sport/Getty Images
Interior Photos: Steph Chambers/Getty Images Sport/Getty Images, 4; AP Images, 7, 17; Mark Rucker/Transcendental Graphics/Getty Images Sport/Getty Images, 9; George Rinhart/Corbis Historical/Getty Images, 11, 12, 15; Bruce Bennett/Getty Images Studios/Getty Images, 18; Focus on Sport/Getty Images, 20, 22, 25; David Durochik/AP Images, 26; John Swart/AP Images, 28; David Madison/Getty Images Sport/Getty Images, 31; Ronald C. Modra/Getty Images Sport/Getty Images, 32; Ben Margot/AP Images, 34, 37; Jim McIsaac/Getty Images Sport/Getty Images, 39; Tony Dejak/AP Images, 40

Editor: Charlie Beattie
Series Designer: Becky Daum

Library of Congress Control Number: 2022940480

Publisher's Cataloging-in-Publication Data

Names: Hewson, Anthony K., author.
Title: Oakland Athletics / by Anthony K. Hewson
Description: Minneapolis, Minnesota: Abdo Publishing, 2023 | Series: Inside MLB | Includes online resources and index.
Identifiers: ISBN 9781098290276 (lib. bdg.) | ISBN 9781098275471 (ebook)
Subjects: LCSH: Oakland Athletics (Baseball team)--Juvenile literature. | Baseball teams--Juvenile literature. | Professional sports--Juvenile literature. | Sports franchises--Juvenile literature. | Major League Baseball (Organization)--Juvenile literature.
Classification: DDC 796.35764--dc23

TABLE OF CONTENTS

A's
Oakland

CHAPTER 1

MADE BY MACK

The Oakland Athletics were cruising. Up 5–0 in Game 2 of the 2020 American League wild-card series, they looked like they were heading to a winner-take-all Game 3. Even though star closer Liam Hendriks gave up a two-run homer in the eighth inning, he was still ready to finish off the game.

Hendriks started off the ninth well. He struck out the first two batters. Then he allowed a pair of singles. The next batter walked to load the bases. Hendriks was done, replaced by Jake Diekman. But Diekman issued another walk. The Sox had the winning run on base. The home crowd was getting nervous. The A's hadn't won a playoff series in 14 years. And that history of losses was all too fresh in everyone's minds.

Jake Diekman delivers a pitch for the Oakland Athletics in a 2020 game.

The next batter was American League (AL) Most Valuable Player (MVP) José Abreu. Diekman focused in. He delivered a fastball. Abreu jumped on it, but he could only manage a ground ball to second. Nate Orf threw to first baseman Matt Olson to finish off the win. The A's championship hopes were still alive.

IN THE BEGINNING

By 2020 the A's had played in Oakland almost as long as they'd played anywhere else. However, Oakland was the team's third home. The Athletics' first 53 years were spent in Philadelphia. It was there that the A's were original members of the AL, which played its first season in 1901.

Philadelphia had been home to other baseball teams dating back to the 1860s. The Phillies of the National League (NL) began playing in 1883. When the Athletics were created by AL president Ban Johnson, he turned to one of the Phillies' owners to run the new team. Sporting goods manufacturer Ben Shibe owned 25 percent of the Phillies. Johnson installed him as the A's main owner.

One of the minority owners was a man named Cornelius McGillicuddy. Better known as Connie Mack, he had been a big-league catcher for 11 seasons. Mack got into managing at the end of his playing career. He was selected to make all

Connie Mack, *right*, shakes the hand of New York Giants manager John McGraw during the 1911 World Series.

the A's baseball decisions, including those on the field as the team's manager.

The AL wanted to rival the established NL. The A's immediately took aim at the Phillies. Mack tried to sign some of their best players. Among the Phillies he brought in was Napoleon Lajoie, one of the best hitters in baseball.

Lajoie hit .426 in 1901, which is still an all-time AL record. But the Phillies got a court order saying the A's didn't have the right to sign Lajoie. Then Mack found out the order was only legal in Pennsylvania. Instead of giving Lajoie back, Mack traded him to a team in Cleveland. With Lajoie in Ohio, the Pennsylvania courts couldn't do anything. The Phillies never got their star back.

THE FIRST DYNASTY

The A's still had one of the best teams in the AL without Lajoie. They won their first AL title in 1902. The World Series did not exist until the following year. But the Athletics would get their chance soon enough.

Ace pitcher Rube Waddell led the AL in wins, earned-run average (ERA), and strikeouts in 1905. The rotation also included two more future Hall of Famers in Eddie Plank and Charles Bender. The 1905 A's won the AL and made their first World Series but lost in five games to the New York Giants.

In 1909 the A's opened one of the greatest ballparks in the country. At the time, wooden ballparks were common. The Athletics' new Shibe Park was

THE WHITE ELEPHANT

As the A's were signing stars like Napoleon Lajoie in their early years, a reporter asked New York Giants manager John McGraw what he thought about that. McGraw was unimpressed, saying the A's were a "white elephant." A white elephant is a term for a prize that is not actually valuable. Connie Mack decided to have fun with it and make an elephant the A's mascot. They still use it today.

instead constructed of steel and concrete. It had two decks, and owner Ben Shibe kept ticket prices low to ensure anyone who wanted to come to the ballpark could afford to attend a game.

Rube Waddell led the AL in strikeouts every year from 1902 to 1907.

Fans who came out saw some of the era's best players. Second baseman Eddie Collins and third baseman Frank Baker were future Hall of Famers. Shortstop Jack Barry was also a star. The A's won the AL in 1910 with a team-record 102 wins. In the World Series, Philadelphia's bats overwhelmed the NL champion Chicago Cubs. Collins and Baker each had nine hits in the five-game series. The A's outscored Chicago 35–15. Pitcher Jack Coombs won three games as the team captured its first World Series title.

Philadelphia was even better in 1911. The team added first baseman John "Stuffy" McInnis. Along with Collins, Barry, and Baker, he made up what was known as "the $100,000 Infield."

The A's again won more than 100 games in 1911 and made the World Series. It was a rematch of the 1905 series against the Giants. Before it started, Baker had no nickname. But then he hit the winning home run in Game 2. In Game 3, he hit a game-tying shot. After Philadelphia won in six games, the A's third baseman was forever known as "Home Run" Baker.

The $100,000 Infield won one more title together as they made it back to the World Series in 1913, where they once again faced the Giants. Pitching again led the way as Bender won in both of his starts. Plank was on the mound for the clinching game this time, allowing just two hits. And Baker drove in the winning runs in a 3–1 victory for the A's third title in four years.

BENDER

Charles Bender was one of the few Indigenous MLB stars in the early 1900s. A member of the Ojibwa Nation, Bender had to deal with constant racism during his career. Fans from opposing dugouts frequently taunted him. And many around baseball insisted on giving him the nickname "Chief." Bender rose above the discrimination to post 212 wins and a 2.46 career ERA in 16 seasons. Mack called him the best "big game" pitcher he had ever seen.

END OF AN ERA

The A's seemed like they could contend for several more championships. The 1914 team cruised to another AL title. After coming close to winning AL MVP honors in the previous three years, Collins finally took home the award. The A's squared off with the Boston Braves in the World Series.

Frank "Home Run" Baker hit 48 of his 96 career home runs while playing for the Philadelphia Athletics.

To the surprise of many, Boston won in a sweep. It was the final run for the A's. The Federal League, a new rival to MLB, came after Mack's stars with high-salary offers. The A's manager couldn't match them. So he broke up the team completely, selling Collins to the Chicago White Sox for a record price of $50,000. Baker was gone by the end of 1914. Over the next two years, the A's won only 79 total games. It was time for Mack to build the team back up again.

CHAPTER 2

A SECOND DYNASTY

As part owner of the team, Connie Mack was sure he had time to rebuild the A's as a winner. And doing so took a while. The team remained one of the worst in baseball for nearly 10 years.

Mack was the team's steady presence. Wearing his signature full suit and tie, he was always visible in the dugout. Managers today must wear the team's uniform. And they also can't own any portion of the team. Mack was one of the last of his kind in baseball.

Mack's long rebuilding plan started to come together in the late 1920s. The A's lineup once again featured a handful of future Hall of Famers. Outfielder Al Simmons could hit for

Al Simmons hit a franchise-record .356 during his 12 seasons with the Athletics.

average and power. First baseman Jimmie Foxx was a feared slugger who won two MVPs with the A's. Mickey Cochrane was one of the best offensive catchers ever to play.

The A's also had an ace pitcher in Robert "Lefty" Grove. From 1925 to 1931, Grove led the AL in strikeouts every year. He too would end up in the Hall of Fame.

Even with all those stars, competing in the AL during the 1920s was a tough task. The league was ruled by the powerful New York Yankees. Their "Murderers' Row" lineup of sluggers included legends Babe Ruth and Lou Gehrig. The 1927 A's won 91 games. Yet they finished 19 games behind New York.

The A's got a little closer in 1928 behind an MVP season from Cochrane. Then in 1929 they won a team-record 104 games and ran away with the AL pennant. The Chicago Cubs awaited in the World Series.

THE SPITE FENCE

Like many old ballparks, Shibe Park was located in a residential neighborhood. Fans who lived across the street from the outfield fences could look in and see the action. Some even built seats on their roofs and sold tickets. Eventually the A's got tired of this and added on to the existing fence. The addition made it 50 feet (15 m) high and put an end to the free show.

BACK ON TOP

Foxx hit a home run to give the A's the lead in their Game 1 win. Simmons joined Foxx going

Pitcher Lefty Grove won at least 20 games every year from 1927 to 1933 for the A's.

deep in Game 2 as the A's won again. After a 3–1 Game 3 loss, they took a 2–1 series lead into Game 4 in Philadelphia.

The Cubs jumped out to an 8–0 lead heading into the bottom of the seventh inning. But then the A's big bats started teeing off on Cubs starter Charlie Root. Simmons led off the seventh with a homer. Each of the next four batters followed with hits. When the dust had settled, Philadelphia had sent

15 batters to the plate and scored 10 runs. The A's won 10–8 and then closed out the series with a thrilling 3–2 win in Game 5.

Just as he had 20 years earlier, Mack built a team capable of repeating. The 1930 A's again won more than 100 games on their way to the pennant. And again, they emerged victorious in the World Series. Behind the stellar pitching of Grove and George Earnshaw, the A's topped the St. Louis Cardinals in six games. The biggest moment came when Foxx broke a scoreless tie in the ninth inning of Game 5. With Cochrane on base, Foxx drilled a two-run homer into the seats at Sportsman's Park in St. Louis. The runs held up, and Earnshaw closed out the series two days later by striking out six in a 7–1 complete game win.

CONNIE'S FAREWELL

The 1931 A's bested their team record with 107 wins. Grove was MVP as he went 31–4. But Philadelphia stumbled in a World Series with the Cardinals. This time St. Louis won in seven games.

As he had years earlier, Mack started selling off his high-priced stars. Simmons went to the Chicago White Sox after the 1932 season. Cochrane and Grove left on the same day in 1933. Cochrane went to the Detroit Tigers and Grove to the Boston Red Sox. Foxx hung on through 1935 before he was

Jimmie Foxx, *far right*, is congratulated at home plate during the 1931 World Series.

also shipped to the Red Sox. The A's began to tumble down the AL standings.

Ben Shibe had passed away in 1922. Over time Mack purchased more shares of the team to become its majority owner. But he was also 73 years old in 1935. Some wondered if he had what it took to get the A's back to winning.

A third-place finish in 1933 turned out to be the team's best for more than three decades. The A's now often finished last. Mack remained manager into his 80s, and players started to notice his age. Mack would fall asleep in the dugout and forget their names.

Shibe Park, later renamed Connie Mack Stadium, was the home of the Philadelphia Athletics for 46 years.

Mack finally retired in 1950, at age 87. He had managed the A's for 50 years. His 3,731 wins were nearly 1,000 more than second place. Those records are unlikely to be broken. But his time had passed.

Without Mack, the A's got better almost immediately. The 1952 team had a winning record and an MVP season from pitcher Bobby Shantz. But off the field, the A's were struggling to earn money.

Mack's sons Roy and Earle had since taken over control of the team. To do so, they took on heavy loans. However, they struggled to repay their debts and in 1954 were forced to sell the team. The buyer, Arnold Johnson, chose to move the A's to Kansas City, Missouri.

HEADING WEST

Johnson had sports ownership experience. He had once been the owner of Yankee Stadium. Johnson gave that up when he bought the A's, but his new team still had ties to the Yankees. Johnson traded several young stars to New York, often for older veterans. As a result, the Kansas City A's were frequently a last-place team while the Yankees continued to dominate baseball.

Johnson died in 1960, and Charles Finley bought the team. Finley worked hard to promote the A's and generate fan interest. Some of his stranger promotions included a mechanical rabbit that delivered balls to the umpire and a live mule as a mascot. Those gimmicks distracted from

GREEN WITH ENVY

Charles Finley was responsible for the Athletics' change to green and gold uniforms in 1963. The team previously wore red, white, and blue. Not everyone was happy with the change. The team's only All-Star in 1963, Norm Siebern, never got in the game. That was because AL manager Ralph Houk thought the uniforms were so ugly.

New owner Charles Finley considered Louisville, Dallas, and Atlanta as landing spots before moving the Athletics to Oakland ahead of the 1968 season.

the play on the field. The A's had losing records in every season in Kansas City.

To make matters worse, the A's never drew many fans in Kansas City. Finley began looking for a place to move the team. Oakland had just built a new stadium for the Raiders football team. Finley chose California and announced the move just days after the 1967 season ended. The A's were on the move once again.

A PERFECT START

Despite more than a decade of losing while playing in Kansas City, the A's arrived in California in good shape. During the 1960s, the franchise developed a strong minor league system. The team brought up three future Hall of Famers in pitchers Jim "Catfish" Hunter and Rollie Fingers, plus slugger Reggie Jackson. Future All-Stars like pitcher Vida Blue, shortstop Bert Campaneris, and third baseman Sal Bando also came through the team's system.

On May 8, 1968, Hunter took the mound in Oakland and retired all 27 Minnesota Twins he faced. It was just the ninth perfect game in MLB history. And it was a sign that Oakland had a club on the rise.

A's
A's

CHAPTER 3

GREENER PASTURES

The A's finally broke through in Oakland during the 1971 season. The team won 101 games, and Vida Blue won both MVP and the Cy Young Award, given to the best pitcher in each league. Two years earlier, baseball had introduced a new playoff round. Despite the great season, Oakland did not make the World Series. The A's lost to an equally strong Baltimore Orioles team in the AL Championship Series (ALCS).

A year later, Oakland made it through the ALCS—but just barely. The A's needed the full five games to knock off the Detroit Tigers and make it back to the World Series. Their opponents were the mighty Cincinnati Reds.

Catfish Hunter was an All-Star twice when the team played in Kansas City and four more times in Oakland.

Both teams were loaded with future Hall of Famers. But they couldn't have looked more different. The straightlaced Reds were one of many teams that forced players to shave. But by 1972, outrageous beards, mustaches, and sideburns were signature looks for several Oakland A's. Owner Charles Finley was normally very tight with money. Most of the players disliked him because he paid them low salaries. But Finley offered up bonuses to grow out their facial hair. The press dubbed the series "the Hairs vs. the Squares."

Unfortunately for the A's, Reggie Jackson was injured during the ALCS. Oakland would have to beat the Reds without one of the league's best power hitters.

Instead, it was the A's pitchers who took command against the Reds. Led by Catfish Hunter and lefty Ken Holtzman, Oakland held Cincinnati to two runs or fewer in five of seven games. The bad news was that the A's didn't score more than four runs in any

HAMMER TIME

One of the clubhouse attendants for the A's championship teams of the 1970s was a young boy named Stanley Burrell. He earned the nickname "Hammer" after the great slugger Hank Aaron. Oakland's players thought Burrell looked like Aaron. In the late 1980s, Burrell rose to fame as a musician, calling himself "MC Hammer." With hit songs like "U Can't Touch This" and "2 Legit 2 Quit," Burrell has sold more than 50 million records.

game either. The result was a tense seven-game series in which six of the games were decided by a single run.

Gene Tenace hit only five home runs in the 1972 regular season before slugging four in the World Series.

Oakland's secret weapon turned out to be catcher/first baseman Gene Tenace. Up until that season, the fourth-year major leaguer had mainly been a backup. During the season, he hit only five home runs in 82 games. In the World Series, Tenace slugged four homers and drove in nine of Oakland's 16 runs.

In the sixth inning of Game 7, Tenace came up with a runner on in a 1–1 tie. He ripped a double down the left-field line to score Bert Campaneris. Sal Bando then doubled in Tenace's replacement, pinch runner Allan Lewis. The runs held up in a 3–2 victory. It was Oakland's first title in any major professional sport.

Reggie Jackson's ability to produce in the playoffs earned him the nickname "Mr. October."

DEFENDING THE CROWN

Just like the old Philadelphia Athletics under Connie Mack, the new Oakland version was built to win multiple titles. Led by manager Dick Williams, Oakland won 94 games in 1973 and topped the AL West. Healthy again, Jackson socked 32 home runs and was named AL MVP.

After beating the Orioles in the ALCS, Oakland took on the New York Mets in the World Series. New York entered Game 6 in Oakland with a 3–2 lead. Then Jackson started displaying the clutch hitting that would eventually earn him the nickname "Mr. October." He had two run-scoring doubles off Mets ace Tom Seaver in Game 6. That was all the run support Hunter needed as he held New York to one run over 7 1/3 innings. His third win of the postseason forced Game 7.

The A's came out roaring in the final game. Both Campaneris and Jackson hit two-run home runs in the bottom of the third inning. Jackson's blast was his ninth hit of the series. After the A's won 5–2 for their second straight title, the outfielder was named series MVP.

FINLEY'S FIRE SALE

Hunter had his best season yet in 1974. He won the Cy Young Award after leading the league in wins and ERA. In Game 1 of the World Series against the Los Angeles Dodgers, Hunter was even called on to pitch the ninth and preserve an A's win. The right-hander then started Game 3 and gave the A's a 2–1 series lead. However, it was Rollie Fingers who earned series MVP honors for his dominance in locking down the ends of games. That included Game 5, when he pitched shutout innings in the eighth and ninth. Oakland celebrated once more as the A's finished off a third title in a row.

However, the fun didn't last long. By this time, the players were tired of Finley's penny-pinching ways. Hunter took advantage of a loophole to get out of his contract after 1974 and signed with the New York Yankees. Free agency came to MLB after the 1975 season. Many of the A's knew they could get better contracts elsewhere. Finley decided he would rather trade the rest of his best players than lose them for nothing.

By 1977 he had shipped all his World Series stars elsewhere. That year Oakland finished nearly 40 games behind the first-place Kansas City Royals.

Finley finally decided to sell the team itself in 1980. Local businessman Walter Haas went to work rebuilding the A's once again.

Rickey Henderson holds up his record-setting 119th stolen base of the season on August 27, 1982.

BASH BROTHERS AND BEYOND

It took several years for Oakland to contend again. But in 1982, A's fans came to the park just to watch outfielder Rickey Henderson steal bases. The ultraconfident Henderson was on a record-breaking pace that season. The old stolen-base record was 118. Henderson broke it on August 27, with a month to go. He finished with 130.

Even with Henderson swiping bags, the A's still had a losing record. After two more sub-.500 seasons, Henderson was traded to the Yankees.

Instead, the core of the 1980s A's featured a pair of fierce sluggers. José Canseco and Mark McGwire were big and strong and could punish a baseball. Their post–home run celebration saw them slap meaty forearms together. It earned them the nickname "Bash Brothers."

General manager Sandy Alderson built the rest of the team around his sluggers. Several A's were veterans looking for a second chance. Pitcher Dave Stewart had failed a 1986 tryout with the Orioles. In Oakland he became an All-Star.

Pitcher Dennis Eckersley was traded to the A's for minor league prospects. The former starter became a standout reliver in Oakland. Starting pitcher Mike Moore had a losing record with the Seattle Mariners. But he found great success in Oakland. Moore won 19 games in his first season with the A's and made his only All-Star team.

BATTLING FOR THE BAY

In 1988 Canseco was the AL MVP as the A's reached the World Series. There they were upset by the Los Angeles Dodgers. In 1989 Canseco was limited to 65 games. It didn't matter for Oakland. Canseco still hit 17 home runs. McGwire added a team-high 33. Veteran designated hitter Dave Parker picked up the slack by hitting 22 more.

On the mound, Stewart led a dominant staff. Four starters won at least 17 games. And in midseason, Alderson brought Henderson back from the Yankees. He stole 52 bases in 85 games with Oakland. It all added up to a 99-win season for manager Tony La Russa. The A's then brushed aside the Toronto Blue Jays in a five-game ALCS.

Oakland's World Series opponents were much closer to home. Just across the San Francisco Bay, the NL champs were the San Francisco Giants. Oakland was a heavy favorite. That was even more true when Stewart pitched a five-hit Game 1 shutout. Moore followed up with seven dominant innings as Oakland took the second game 5–1.

Then everything changed. As the teams warmed up for Game 3, a major earthquake struck California's Bay Area. Nobody was hurt inside the stadium, but there was major damage throughout both cities. The Bay Bridge, which links San Francisco and Oakland, collapsed. More than 60 people were killed.

The World Series was shut down for 10 days as the area recovered. The time to rest also meant the A's could bring Stewart and Moore back to start the next two games. Oakland won both in convincing fashion. The series was a rout, but it

Dennis Eckersley became one of baseball's best closers after joining the A's.

was remembered more for the devastating earthquake than for what happened on the field. Years later the series win came with another black mark. Both Canseco and McGwire admitted to taking performance-enhancing drugs (PEDs).

Henderson won MVP in 1990, but the A's could not repeat. They were upset in the World Series by the Reds. A year later, Henderson set the all-time stolen base record.

In 1992 Eckersley won both the Cy Young and MVP Awards. But Oakland failed to get past the Toronto Blue Jays in the ALCS. That group of A's never got another shot as stars left the team or retired. Yet another rebuild began in Oakland.

25

CHAPTER 4

MONEYBALL

The A's didn't do much winning for the rest of the 1990s. Oakland never made much money. And the team could no longer afford to pay the big contracts stars were getting. However, fans could still come out to see Mark McGwire smash home runs. McGwire was one of the few players left from the 1989 World Series team.

In 1996 McGwire led the AL with 52 homers. The 1997 season was his last under contract with the A's. Instead of signing him to a new deal, the A's traded him to the St. Louis Cardinals. The A's got back minor leaguers who never made an impact in the majors. McGwire went on to break the single-season home run record in 1998.

Mark McGwire's 363 home runs are an Athletics franchise record.

Trading McGwire was one of the last moves made by general manager Sandy Alderson. After the season, the team promoted assistant Billy Beane to general manager. Beane, who had once been a team scout, would change the A's, and baseball, forever.

WINNING WITH NUMBERS

Beane had been a former player who had spent parts of six seasons in the big leagues. After retiring as a player, he joined the A's staff under Alderson. There he learned an advanced kind of statistical analysis called analytics.

Barry Zito went 23–5 for the A's on his way to winning the 2002 AL Cy Young Award.

All baseball teams looked closely at player statistics. But teams in the late 1990s still mostly chose players based on in-person observations from scouts. The idea of analytics was to find players who might not look like stars but whose statistics showed they could help teams win. And the kind of statistics mattered. Teams at the time valued stats like batting average. However, analysis showed those stats were not all that useful.

Successfully using analytics was huge for a team like the A's. If they could find players who other teams missed, they wouldn't have to compete for high-priced players. Writer Michael Lewis spent time with the team while the general manager tried this theory out. Lewis made Beane and the A's famous with his book *Moneyball*. Soon other teams caught on. Today, all MLB teams use analytics in some way.

Beane's first A's teams had some of the lowest player salaries in baseball. They looked for players who could get on base and hit for power. If runners were often on base and hitters could hit home runs, that was an easy way to score.

The A's slowly developed into one of the best teams in baseball. Oakland had superstars like Jason Giambi, Miguel Tejada, and Eric Chávez. But the "Moneyball" approach unearthed hidden gems like first baseman

MOVIE STARS

The success of Billy Beane and the A's was well known to baseball fans. It became known to movie fans as well in 2011 when *Moneyball* was turned into a film. Brad Pitt was nominated for an Academy Award for his portrayal of Beane. The movie also received five other nominations.

Scott Hatteberg and reliever Chad Bradford. Oakland also had great starting pitching. Tim Hudson, Mark Mulder, and future Cy Young winner Barry Zito were one of the best pitching trios in MLB.

GOLDEN AGE OF MONEYBALL

Giambi was MVP in 2000 as the A's returned to the playoffs. They faced the Yankees, who had a combined team salary of $113 million. Oakland's was $33 million. Despite that, the A's pushed the series to the maximum five games before losing. The same result happened in 2001.

Moneyball worked well to find players. But keeping those players was then the challenge. Oakland still couldn't pay top salaries. As a result, Giambi signed to the Yankees after the 2001 season.

Still, the A's kept right on winning. The 2002 team at one point rattled off 20 wins in a row. That was an AL record. The A's were drawing crowds not seen since their World Series days.

One trend was becoming clear, however. The A's were enjoying regular-season success. They just couldn't quite get the job done in the playoffs. The A's lost in the AL Division Series (ALDS) in five games each season from 2000 to 2003.

The team kept losing more stars. They had to constantly keep finding new, young talent. Hudson and Mulder were each

Teammates mob Scott Hatteberg (10) after his walk-off home run extends Oakland's AL-record winning streak to 20 games on September 4, 2002.

traded after 2004. Getting future All-Star Dan Haren in return for Mulder helped keep the team going.

Oakland finally broke through with a sweep of the Minnesota Twins in the ALDS in 2006. But the A's were then swept in the ALCS. It took six more years for Oakland to get back to the playoffs.

A NEW DIRECTION

The A's continued to rely heavily on analytics. And they continued to function with a small player payroll. But the core of the Moneyball era was all gone by the 2010s.

In 2012 the A's added star outfielders Yoenis Céspedes and Josh Reddick. The pair combined for 55 home runs and led Oakland back to the playoffs. But once again the team didn't make it past the ALDS.

Manager Bob Melvin proved to be a steady leader for the A's. But the roster kept changing. Players who became stars often didn't stick around long. Slugging third baseman Josh Donaldson left after the 2014 season. The next year he won AL MVP as a Toronto Blue Jay. Reddick left and won a World Series with the Houston Astros.

Despite that, the A's were usually a playoff team. They just were unable to win a series. Meanwhile, the team played in the aging Oakland Coliseum. The 2017 season was the 50th in the Coliseum for the A's. The team's ownership felt that the stadium needed replacing if the A's were going to make enough money to stay competitive.

The 2020 A's were coming off back-to-back losses in the AL wild-card game. They won the division in 2020 and faced the Chicago White Sox in the AL wild-card series. After rescuing a win in Game 2, the A's faced a winner-take-all Game 3.

Josh Donaldson hit 53 home runs and drove in 191 runs over two seasons while helping the A's reach the playoffs in both 2013 and 2014.

First baseman Matt Olson was one of the many stars the A's traded away after the 2021 season, as the future of the team in Oakland was up in the air.

After falling behind 3–0 early, Oakland rallied back to take a 4–3 lead. Chicago quickly tied the game back up. In the bottom of the fifth, light-hitting Oakland third baseman Chad Pinder hit a two-run single. That was all the A's needed. The 6–4 win clinched the team's first playoff series victory in 14 years.

Players from that team such as first baseman Matt Olson and pitcher Sean Manaea turned into stars in 2021. But as with stars for the entire history of the franchise, both were traded before the 2022 season. That left the A's with an uncertain future on the field.

Their future off the diamond was even more uncertain as the team tried to find a way to build a new stadium. Fans hoped for more World Series memories like in the 1970s and 1980s. And they hoped to make those memories in Oakland.

TIMELINE

1901

The Philadelphia Athletics join the American League in its inaugural season.

1905

The A's make their first World Series appearance but lose to the New York Giants.

1910

Behind strong pitching performances, the A's win their first World Series, defeating the Chicago Cubs in five games.

1913

The A's win their third championship in four years by beating the Giants 4–1.

1929

Stars Mickey Cochrane, Jimmie Foxx, and Al Simmons lead Philadelphia to its first World Series title in 16 years by beating the Chicago Cubs 4–1.

1930

The A's return to the World Series for a second consecutive season and beat the St. Louis Cardinals 4–2.

1950

After 50 seasons and more than 3,000 wins, manager and owner Connie Mack retires.

1954

Facing financial problems, the A's are sold to Arnold Johnson, who moves the team to Kansas City.

1960

Charles Finley buys the A's following Johnson's death and begins working on promoting the team while also considering a move elsewhere.

1967

Finley announces after the season the team is moving to Oakland, California.

1972

Led by Gene Tenace's nine RBIs, the A's defeat the Cincinnati Reds and win the World Series.

1974

The A's win their third championship in a row by beating the Los Angeles Dodgers.

1989

In a series interrupted by a massive earthquake, the A's sweep the San Francisco Giants for their first World Series title in 15 years.

1997

The A's hire Billy Beane as general manager. Beane employs a new form of statistical analysis to overhaul the team's player evaluation process.

2006

After four first-round losses, the A's win their first playoff series under Beane with a three-game sweep of the Minnesota Twins.

2020

The A's win a second playoff series under Beane with a 2–1 series win over the Chicago White Sox.

TEAM FACTS

FRANCHISE HISTORY

Philadelphia Athletics (1901–54)
Kansas City Athletics (1955–67)
Oakland Athletics (1968–)

WORLD SERIES CHAMPIONSHIPS

1910, 1911, 1913, 1929, 1930, 1972, 1973, 1974, 1989

KEY PLAYERS

Mickey Cochrane (1925–33)
Eddie Collins (1906–14, 1927–30)
Jimmie Foxx (1925–35)
Lefty Grove (1925–33)
Rickey Henderson (1979–84, 1989–93, 1994–95, 1998)
Jim "Catfish" Hunter (1965–74)
Reggie Jackson (1967–75, 1987)
Mark McGwire (1986–97)
Eddie Plank (1901–14)
Al Simmons (1924–32, 1940–41, 1944)
Barry Zito (2000–06, 2015)

KEY MANAGERS

Tony La Russa (1986–95)
Connie Mack (1901–50)
Bob Melvin (2011–21)
Dick Williams (1971–73)

HOME STADIUMS

Columbia Park (1901–08)
Connie Mack Stadium (1909–54)
Also known as:
Shibe Park (1909–52)
Municipal Stadium (1955–67)
RingCentral Coliseum (1968–)
Also known as:
Oakland-Alameda County Coliseum (1968–98)
Network Associates Coliseum (1998–2004)
McAfee Coliseum (2004–08)
Oakland Coliseum (2009–11, 2016–18)
O.co Coliseum (2011–15)

TEAM TRIVIA

MR. SPEED

Herb Washington played 105 games in 1974 and 1975 but never got to bat. The former sprinter was signed just to steal bases, and he nabbed 31 of them in those two seasons.

ANYBODY HOME?

The A's struggled with attendance in a disappointing 1979 season. The low point was an April game for which the team sold just 653 tickets.

SIGNATURE CLEATS

Among many A's uniform firsts, the team switched to white shoes in their final season in Kansas City. While other teams wear black shoes, the A's have kept their signature look ever since.

DESERT BASEBALL

In 1996 Oakland Coliseum was undergoing renovations. The A's opened the season instead in Las Vegas at Cashman Field. It marked the first time major league games were played in a minor league stadium since 1957.

GLOSSARY

ace

A team's best starting pitcher.

closer

A pitcher who comes in at the end of the game to secure a win for his team.

contract

An agreement to play for a certain team.

free agency

A period after the season when free agents are allowed to sign with new teams.

general manager

An executive who runs a team and is responsible for finding and signing players.

loophole

A detail of the wording in a rule that allows a person to get around following that rule.

minor league

A lower level of baseball at which players work on improving their skills before they reach the major leagues.

perfect game

A complete game in which a team retires every opposing batter and allows no base runners.

shutout

A complete game in which a team allows no runs.

upset

An unexpected victory by a supposedly weaker team or player.

veteran

A player who has played many years.

MORE INFORMATION

BOOKS

Flynn, Brendan. *The MLB Encyclopedia*. Minneapolis, MN: Abdo Publishing, 2022.

Gitlin, Marty. *MLB*. Minneapolis, MN: Abdo Publishing, 2021.

Mitchell, Bo. *Ultimate MLB Road Trip*. Minneapolis, MN: Abdo Publishing, 2019.

ONLINE RESOURCES

To learn more about the Oakland Athletics, please visit **abdobooklinks.com** or scan this QR code. These links are routinely monitored and updated to provide the most current information available.

INDEX

ABOUT THE AUTHOR

Anthony K. Hewson is a freelance writer who specializes in writing nonfiction for kids.